English/German

Picture Dictionary

More than 325 Essential Words

Dylanna Press

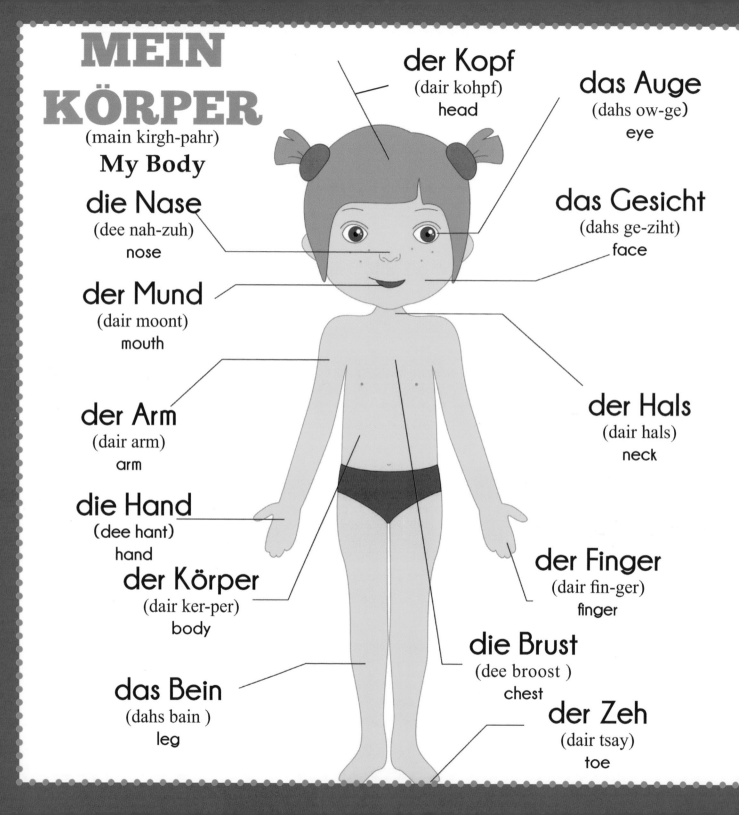

MEIN KÖRPER
(main kirgh-pahr)
My Body

der Kopf
(dair kohpf)
head

das Auge
(dahs ow-ge)
eye

das Gesicht
(dahs ge-ziht)
face

die Nase
(dee nah-zuh)
nose

der Mund
(dair moont)
mouth

der Hals
(dair hals)
neck

der Arm
(dair arm)
arm

die Hand
(dee hant)
hand

der Körper
(dair ker-per)
body

der Finger
(dair fin-ger)
finger

die Brust
(dee broost)
chest

das Bein
(dahs bain)
leg

der Zeh
(dair tsay)
toe

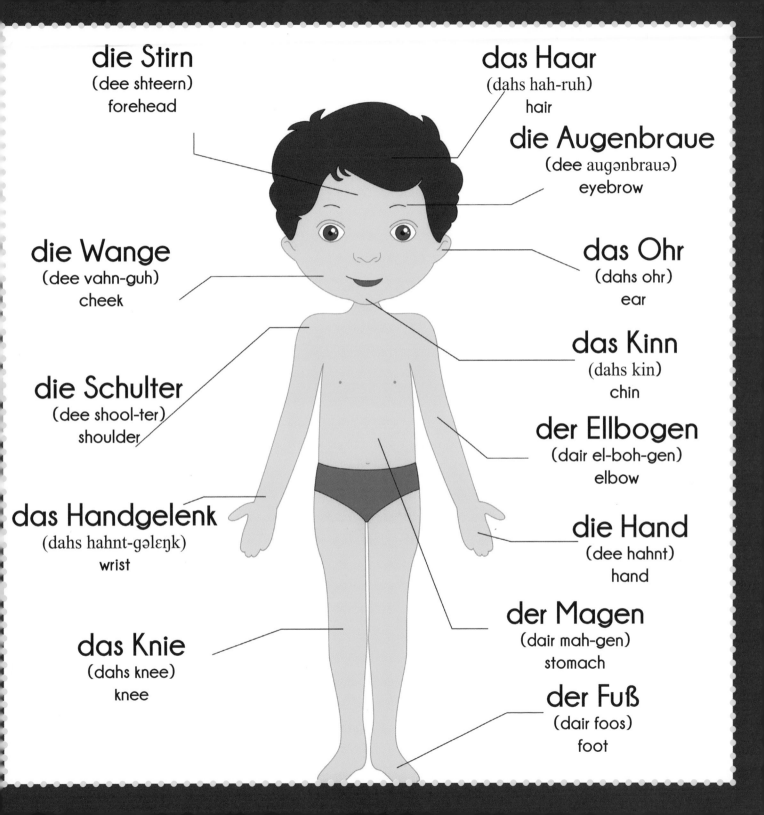

die Familie
(dee fah-mee-lee-eh)

Family

der Bruder
(dair broo-der)
brother

die Mutter
(dee moot-ter)
mother

der Großvater
(dair grohs-fah-ter)
grandfather

der Onkel
(dair ohn-kel)
uncle

die Großmutter
(dee grohs-moot-ter)
grandmother

die Tante
(dee tahn-tuh)
aunt

die Schwester
(dee shves-ter)
sister

der Vater
(dair fah-ter)
father

die Kusine
(dee koo-zee-nuh)
cousin

der Cousin
(dair koo-zeen)
cousin

mein Haus
(main hows)

my house

das Wohnzimmer
(dahs vohn-tsim-mer)

living room

die Küche
(dee ku-huh)

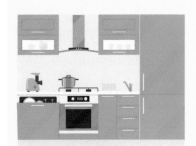

kitchen

das Schlafzimmer
(dahs shlahf-tsim-mer)

bedroom

das Badezimmer
(dahs bah-de-tsim-mer)

bathroom

die Treppe
(dee trep-puh)

stairs

das Fenster
(dahs fen-ster)

window

der Kamin
(dair kah-meen)

fireplace

die Tür
(dee tur)

door

die Couch
(dee kautʃ)

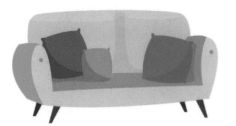

couch

der Stuhl
(dair shtoohl)

chair

der Tisch
(dair tish)

table

die Lampe
(dee lahm-puh)

lamp

das Fernsehen
(dahs fairn-zay-er)

television

die Frisierkommode
(dee fri-zeer-kohm-moh-duh)

dresser

das Pult
(dair poolt)

desk

das Bücherregal
(dahs bu-her-ray-gahl)

bookcase

der Hocker
(dair hohk-ker)

stool

im Schlafzimmer

(im shlahf-tsim-mer)

In the bedroom

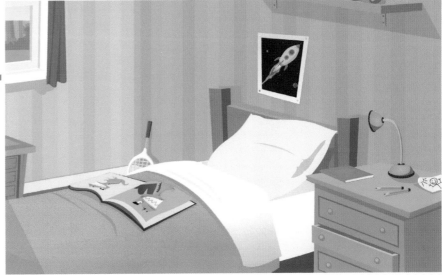

das Bett
(dahs bet)

bed

das Kissen
(dahs kis-sehn)

pillow

die Decke
(dee dek-kuh)

blanket

der Kleiderschrank
(dair kligh-der-shrahnk)

wardrobe

die Uhr
(dee oor)

clock

der Spiegel
(dair shpee-gel)

mirror

die Küche
(dee ku-huh)

kitchen

der Kühlschrank
(dair kuhl-shrahnk)

refrigerator

der Herd
(dair hairt)

stove

die Schüssel
(dee shus-sel)

bowl

die Tasse
(dee tahs-suh)

cup

das Glas
(dahs glahs)

glass

das Schneidebrett
(dahs shnay-de-bret)

cutting board

das Messer
(dahs mes-ser)

knife

die Gabel
(dee gah-bel)

fork

der Wasserkessel
(dair vahs-ser-kes-sel)

kettle

die Pfanne
(dee pfahn-nuh)

pan

der Topf
(dair tohpf)

pot

der Teller
(dair tel-ler)

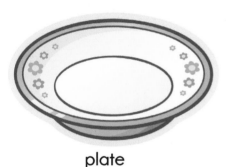

plate

der Löffel
(dair lerf-fel)

spoon

die Teekanne
(dee tay-kah-nuh)

teapot

der Schneebesen
(dair schnay-bes-en)

whisk

die Geschirrspüler
(dee ge-schir-schpoo-ler)

dishwasher

die Mikrowelle
(dee mee-kroh-vel)

microwave

das Badezimmer
(dahs bah-de-tsim-me)

bathroom

die Badewanne
(dee bah-de-vahn-nuh)

bathtub

die Seife
(dee zigh-fuh)

soap

die Bürste
(dee bur-stuh)

brush

die Blasen
(dee blah-zuhn)

bubbles

der Kamm
(dair kahmm)

comb

der Wasserhahn
(dair vahs-ser-hahn)

faucet

die Skala
(dee skah-lah)

scale

das Shampoo
(dahs shahm-poo)

shampoo

die Dusche
(dee doo-shuh)

shower

die Spüle
(dee shpul)

sink

der Schwamm
(dair shvahm)

sponge

das Gewebe
(dahs gehv-ebuh)

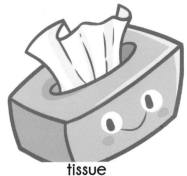

tissue

die Toilette
(dee toy-let-tuh)

toilet

die Zahnbürste
(dee tsahn-bur-stuh)

toothbrush

die Zahnpasta
(dee tsahn-pah-stah)

toothpaste

das Handtuch
(dahs hahnt-took)

towel

das Toilettenpapier
(dahs toy-let-ten-pah-peer)

toilet paper

Meine Kleidung
(main kligh-doong)
My Clothes

der Gürtel
(dair gur-tel)

der Badeanzug
(dair bah-de-ahn-tsook)

die Bluse
(dee bloo-zuh)

belt

swimsuit

blouse

die Stiefel
(dee shtee-fel)

der Mantel
(dair mahn-tel)

das Kleid
(dahs klight)

boots

coat

dress

die Handschuhe
(dee hahnt-shoo-huh)

die Jacke
(dee yahk-kuh)

der Hut
(dair hoot)

gloves

jacket

hat

die Jeans
(dee jeans)

jeans

die Krawatte
(dee krah-vaht-tuh)

necktie

die Hosen
(dee hoh-zen)

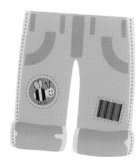

pants

die Overalls
(dee oh-ver-ahls)

overalls

die Handtasche
(dee hahnt-tah-shuh)

purse

die Schlafanzüge
(dee shlaf-ahn-tsook)

pajamas

der Schal
(dair schall)

scarf

die Unterwäsche
(dee oon-ter-vay-shuh)

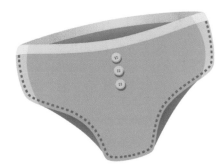

underwear

die Schuhe
(dee shoo-uh)

shoes

der Rock
(dair rohk)

skirt

die Turnschuhe
(dee toorn-shoo-uh)

sneakers

die Socken
(dee zohk-ken)

socks

die Sonnenbrille
(dee zohn-nen-bril-luh)

sunglasses

der Pullover
(dair pool-oh-ver)

sweater

das T-Shirt
(dahs tee-shahrt)

T shirt

die Strumpfhose
(dee shtroompf-hoh-zuh)

tights

die Badehose
(dee bah-de-hoo-zah)

swim trunks

das Sweatshirt
(dahs svet-shirt)

sweatshirt

das Essen
(dahs es-sen)

Food

die Tomate
(dee toh-mah-tuh)

tomato

die Wassermelone
(dee vahs-ser-me-loh-nuh)

watermelon

der Apfel
(dair ahp-fel)

apple

die Orange
(dee oh-rahn-juh)

orange

die Banane
(dee bah-nah-nuh)

banana

die Erdbeeren
(dee aird-bai-ren)

strawberries

die Zitrone
(dee tsi-troh-nuh)

lemon

die Birne
(dee bihr-nuh)

pear

der Salat
(dair zah-laht)

salad

der Käse
(dair kay-zuh)

cheese

das Hühnerfleisch
(dahs hu-ner-flighsh)

chicken

die Lebensmittel
(dee lay-bens-mit-tel)

groceries

die Pfannkuchen
(dee pfahn-kuu-chen)

pancakes

das Sandwich
(dahs zent-vitch)

sandwich

die Spaghetti
(dee schpa-ge-tee)

spaghetti

der Toast
(dair tohst)

toast

der Mais
(dair mighs)

corn

die Butter
(dee boot-ter)

butter

der Reis
(dair righs)

rice

der Kuchen
(dair koo-ken)

cake

die Nüsse
(dee nus-suh)

nuts

das Ei
(dahs eye)

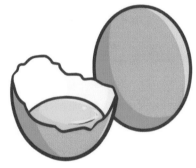

egg

die Kartoffeln
(dee kahr-tohf-feln)

potatoes

das Brot
(dahs broht)

bread

die Pommes
(dee pohm)

chips

die Kekse
(dee playts-hen)

cookies

das Popkorn
(dahs pohp-kohRn)

popcorn

die Pommes frites
(dee pohm frits)

french fries

die Eiscreme
(dee ighs-kr-em)

ice cream

die Karotte
(dee kah-roht)

carrot

die Pizza
(dee pi-tsaa)

pizza

der Brokkoli
(dair brohk-koh-lee)

broccoli

die Milch
(dee milh)

milk

die Zwiebel
(dee tsvee-bel)

onion

der Truthahn
(dair tru-thahn)

turkey

die Tiere
(dee tee-ruh)

Animals

der Vogel
(dair foh-gel)

bird

die Katze
(dee kaht-tsuh)

cat

der Hund
(dair hoont)

dog

die Ente
(dee en-tuh)

duck

der Elefant
(dair e-le-fahnt)

elephant

der Fuchs
(dair fooks)

fox

der Truthahn
(dair tru-thahn)

turkey

der Wal
(dair vahl)

whale

der Panda
(dair pahn-dah)

panda

der Frosch
(dair frohsh)

frog

die Eule
(dee ou-luh)

owl

das Kaninchen
(dahs kahni-nhsh-en)

rabbit

der Hahn
(dair hahn)

rooster

der Affe
(dair ahf-fuh)

monkey

der Löwe
(dair ler-vuh)

lion

der Elch
(dair elk)

moose

das Eichhörnchen
(dahs aich-huhrn-chen)

squirrel

die Schlange
(dee shlahn-guh)

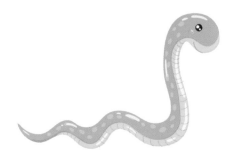

snake

die Maus
(dee mows)

mouse

das Hähnchen
(dahs hu-ner-fliighsh)

chicken

der Alligator
(dair ahl-li-gah-tohR)

alligator

der Bär
(dair bayr)

bear

das Schwein
(dahs shvighn)

pig

die Schildkröte
(dee shilt-krer-tuh)

turtle

das Nilpferd
(dahs ni-lpfe-aht)

hippopotamus

die Giraffe
(dee gee-rahf-fuh)

giraffe

das Kamel
(dahs kah-mel)

camel

der Wolf
(dair vohlf)

wolf

das Zebra
(dahs tsay-brah)

zebra

der Fisch
(dair fish)

fish

die Kuh
(dee koo)

cow

das Schaf
(dahs shahf)

sheep

die Ziege
(dee tsee-guh)

goat

das Pferd
(dahs pfaird)

horse

der Tiger
(dair tee-ger)

tiger

die Schnecke
(dee schne-kuh)

snail

der Pinguin
(dair pin-gu-een)

penguin

der Gorilla
(dair go-ril-lah)

gorilla

die Schule
(dee shoo-luh)

school

der Schulbus
(dair school-boos)

school bus

die Lehrerin
(dee lay-re-rin)

teacher

die Buntstifte
(dee boont-shtift)

crayons

der Klebstoff
(dair klayb-shtoff)

glue

die Notizbücher
(dee noh-teets-boo-cher)

notebooks

die Farbe
(dee fahr-buh)

paint

der Bleistift
(dair bligh-shtift)

pencil

der Globus
(dair gloh-boos)

globe

der Rucksack
(dair rook-zahk)

backpack

der Kugelschreiber
(dair koo-gel-shrigh-ber)

pen

das Lineal
(dahs li-nay-ahl)

ruler

der Rechner
(dair reh-ner)

calculator

die Schere
(dee she-ruh)

scissors

der Tacker
(dair tahk-kahr)

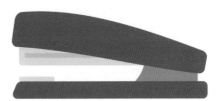

stapler

das Buch
(dahs book)

book

das Pult
(dahs poolt)

desk

die Schülerin
(dee shu-ler-en)

student

das Wetter
(dahs vet-ter)

weather

die Wolke
(dee vohl-kuh)

cloud

der Blitz
(dair blits)

lightning

der Regen
(dair ray-gen)

rain

der Schnee
(dair shnay)

snow

die Sonne
(dee zohn-nuh)

sun

der Tornado
(dair tor-nah-do)

tornado

der Wind
(dair vint)

wind

der Regenbogen
(dair tay-gen-boh-gen)

rainbow

die Jahreszeiten - The Seasons

der Winter
(dair vin-ter)

winter

der Frühling
(dair fru-ling)

spring

der Sommer
(dair sohm-mer)

summer

der Herbst
(dair hairbst)

fall

der Transport
(dair trahns-pohrt)
transportation

das Flugzeug
(ah-byohn)

airplane

der Krankenwagen
(dair krahn-ken-vah-gen)

ambulance

das Fahrrad
(dahs fahr-raht)

bicycle

das Boot
(dahs boht)

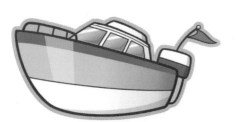

boat

der Bus
(dair boos)

bus

das Auto
(dahs ow-toh)

car

der Feuerwehrauto
(dair foy-er-vair-ow-toh)

firetruck

der Hubschrauber
(dair hoop-shrow-ber)

helicopter

das Motorrad
(dahs moh-tohr-raht)

motorcycle

das Polizeiauto
(dahs poh-li-tsigh-ow-toh)

police car

die Rakete
(dee rah-kay-tuh)

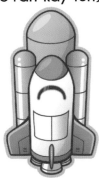

rocket

der Roller
(dair roh-ler)

scooter

das Schiff
(dahs shiff)

ship

das Unterseeboot
(dahs oon-teR-zay-boht)

submarine

der Traktor
(dair trahk-tohr)

tractor

der Zug
(dair tsook)

train

der Lastwagen
(dair lahst-vah-gen)

truck

der Wagen
(dair vah-gen)

wagon

Der Sport - SPORTS
(dair shpohrt)

der Handschuh
(dair hahnt-shoo-huh)

glove

der Baseball
(dair bahs-bahl)

baseball

der Basketball
(dair bahs-ket-bahl)

basketball

das Skateboard
(dahs skate-board)

skateboard

der Tennisschläger
(dair ten-nis-shlay-ger)

tennis racket

der Pfiff
(dair pfif))

whistle

Boxen
(bohk-sen)

boxing

Angeln
(ahn-geln)

fishing

der Fußball
(dair foos-bahl)

football

der Golf
(dair gohlf)

golf

das Schlittschuhlaufen
(dahs shilt-shoo-lau-fen)

skating

das Karate
(dahs ka-raa-te)

karate

der Fußball
(dair foos-bahl)

soccer

das Segeln
(dahs zay-geln)

sailing

das Tennis
(dahs ten-nis)

tennis

das Aktionsverb
(dahs ahkt-seeohn-fairb)
Action Words

kriechen
(krii-chen)

crawl

klettern
(klet-tern)

climb

weinen
(vigh-nen)

cry

trinken
(trin-ken)

drink

essen
(es-sen)

eat

springen
(shprin-gen)

jump

lachen
(lah-hen)

laugh

hören
(herr-enr)

listen

lesen
(lay-zen)

read

laufen
(low-fen)

run

sitzen
(zits-en)

sit

schlafen
(shlah-fen)

sleep

stehen
(schtee-en)

stand

reden
(ray-den)

talk

gehen
(gay-en)

walk

flüstern
(flu-stern)

whisper

umarmen
(oo-mahr-men)

hug

prallen
(prah-len)

bounce

die Emotionen - Emotions
(dee emo-tsjo-n)

ängstlich
(ahngst-lih)

afraid

neugierig
(noy-gii-rih)

curious

traurig
(trow-rih)

sad

wütend
(vu-tent)

angry

überrascht
(uh-ber-rascht)

surprised

glücklich
(gluk-lih)

happy

die Gegensätze- OPPOSITES
(dee gee-gene-se-tse)

schmutzig
(shmoot-tsih)

sauber
(zow-ber)

geschlossen
(ge-schlo-sen)

öffnen
(erf-nen)

dirty

clean

closed

open

kalt
(kahlt)

heiß
(highs)

licht
(light)

dunkel
(doon-kel)

cold

hot

light

dark

die Gegensätze - OPPOSITES

alt
(ahlt)

jung
(yoon-guh)

schwer
(shvair)

leicht
(light)

old

young

heavy

light

laut
(lowt)

ruhig
(ruu-ih)

unten
(oon-ten)

oben
(oh-ben)

loud

quiet

down

up

die Gegensätze - OPPOSITES

trocken
(trohk-ken)

nass
(nahs)

weich
(vigh)

hart
(hahrt)

dry

wet

soft

hard

ziehen
(tsee-en)

drücken
(dru-ken)

über
(uh-ber)

unten
(oon-ten)

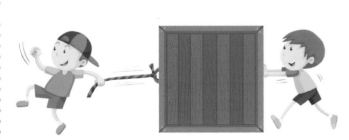

pull

push

above

below

DIE FORMAS - Shapes
(dee fohr-mahs)

der Kreis
(dair krighs)

circle

der Diamant
(dair dia-mant)

diamond

das Rechteck
(dahs reh-tek)

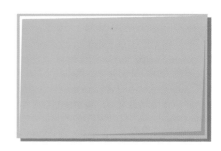

rectangle

das Quadrat
(dahs kva-draht)

square

der Stern
(dair shtair-nuh)

star

das Dreieck
(dahs drigh-ek)

triangle

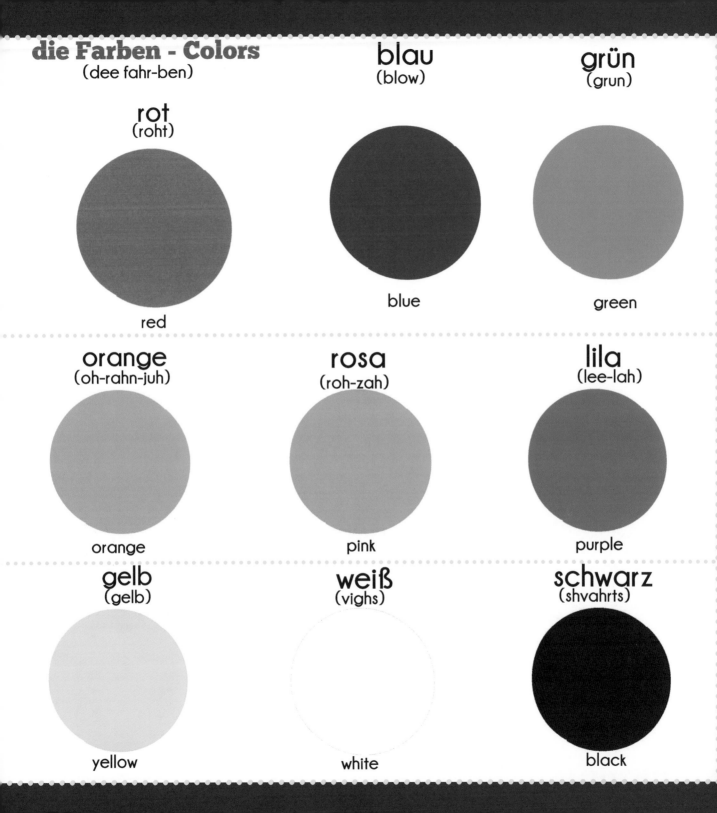

die Farben - Colors
(dee fahr-ben)

rot
(roht)

red

blau
(blow)

blue

grün
(grun)

green

orange
(oh-rahn-juh)

orange

rosa
(roh-zah)

pink

lila
(lee-lah)

purple

gelb
(gelb)

yellow

weiß
(vighs)

white

schwarz
(shvahrts)

black

DIE NUMMERN - Numbers
(dee noom-mern)

eins	zwei	drei	vier	fünf
(ighns)	(tsvigh)	(drigh)	(feer)	(funf)

one

two

three

four

five

sechs	sieben	acht	neun	zehn
(zeks)	(zee-ben)	(axt)	(noyn)	(tsayn)

six

seven

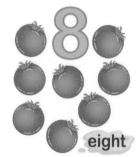
eight

nine

ten

DAS ALPHABET- ALPHABET

(dahs ahl-fah-beet)

A ah	Ä ah Umlaut	B beh	ß ess-tsett	C tseh	D deh	E eh	F eff	G geh	H ha
I ee	J yot	K kah	L ell	M emm	N enn	O oh	Ö oh Umlaut	P peh	Q kuh
R err	S ess	T teh	U uh	Ü uh Umlaut	V fow	W veh	X iks	Y upsilon	Z tsett

German-English Word List

acht	eight	**das Brot**	bread
der Affe	monkey	**der Bruder**	brother
der Alligator	alligator	**die Brust**	chest
alt	old	**das Buch**	book
angeln	fishing	**das Bücherregal**	bookcase
ängstlich	afraid	**die Buntstifte**	crayons
der Apfel	apple	**die Bürste**	brush
der Arm	arm	**der Bus**	bus
blau	blue	**die Butter**	butter
das Alphabet	alphabet	**die Couch**	couch
das Auge	eye	**der Cousin**	cousin
die Augenbraue	eyebrow	**der Diamant**	diamond
das Auto	car	**die Decke**	blanket
der Badeanzug	swimsuit	**drei**	three
die Badehose	swim trunks	**das Dreieck**	triangle
die Badewanne	bathtub	**drücken**	push
das Badezimmer	bathroom	**dunkel**	dark
die Banane	banana	**die Dusche**	shower
der Bär	bear	**das Ei**	egg
der Baseball	baseball	**das Eichhörnchen**	squirrel
der Basketball	basketball	**eins**	one
das Bein	leg	**die Eiscreme**	ice cream
das Bett	bed	**der Elch**	moose
die Bibliothek	library	**der Elefant**	elephant
die Birne	pear	**der Ellbogen**	elbow
die Blasen	bubbles	**die Emotionen**	emotions
der Bleistift	pencil	**die Ente**	duck
der Blitz	lightning	**die Erdbeeren**	strawberries
die Bluse	blouse	**essen**	eating
das Boot	boat	**das Essen**	food
boxen	boxing	**die Eule**	owl
der Brokkoli	broccoli	**das Fahrrad**	bicycle

German-English Word List

die Familie	family	der Großvater	grandfather
die Farbe	paint	dee Großmutter	grandmother
die Farben	colors	grün	green
das Fenster	window	der Hahn	rooster
der Fernseher	television	der Gürtel	belt
das Feuerwehrauto	fire truck	die Haare	hair
der Finger	finger	der Hals	neck
der Fisch	fish	die Hand	hand
flüstern	whisper	das Handgelenk	wrist
die Formen	shapes	der Handschuh	glove
die Frisierkommode	dresser	die Handtasche	purse
der Frosch	frog	das Handtuch	towel
der Frühling	spring	hart	hard
der Fuchs	fox	das Haus	house
der Fuß	foot	heiß	hot
der Fußball	football	das Hemd	shirt
der Fußball	soccer	der Herbst	autumn
fünf	five	der Herd	stove
die Gabel	fork	der Hocker	stool
die Gegensätze	opposites	hören	listening
gehen	walking	die Hosen	pants
gelb	yellow	der Hubschrauber	helicopter
die Geschirrspüler	dishwasher	das Hühnerfleisch	chicken
geschlossen	closed	der Hund	dog
das Gesicht	face	der Hut	hat
das Gewebe	tissue	die Jacke	jacket
die Giraffe	giraffe	die Jahreszeiten	seasons
das Glas	glass	die Jeans	jeans
der Globus	globe	jung	young
glücklich	happy	kalt	cold
golf	golf	das Kamel	camel
der Gorilla	gorilla	der Kamin	fireplace

German-English Word List

der Kamm	comb	die Lebensmittel	groceries
das Kaninchen	rabbit	die Lehrerin	teacher
Karate	karate	leicht	light
die Karotte	carrot	lesen	read
die Kartoffeln	potatoes	licht	light
der Käse	cheese	lila	purple
die Katze	cat	das Lineal	ruler
das Kinn	chin	der Löffel	spoon
der Klebstoff	glue	der Löwe	lion
der Kleiderschrank	wardrobe	der Magen	stomach
klettern	climbing	der Mais	corn
das Kissen	pillow	der Mantel	coat
das Kleid	dress	die Maus	mouse
die Kleidung	clothes	das Messer	knife
das Knie	knee	die Mikrowelle	microwave
der Kopf	head	die Milch	milk
der Körper	body	das Motorrad	motorcycle
der Krankenwagen	ambulance	der Mund	mouth
die Krawatte	necktie	die Mutter	mother
der Kreis	circle	die Nase	nose
kriechen	crawling	nass	wet
die Küche	kitchen	neugierig	curious
der Kuchen	cake	neun	nine
der Kugelschreiber	pen	das Nilpferd	hippopotamus
die Kuh	cow	die Notizbücher	notebooks
der Kühlschrank	refrigerator	die Nummern	numbers
die Kusine	cousin (female)	die Nüsse	nuts
lachen	laugh	oben	up
die Lampe	lamp	öffnen	open
der Lastwagen	truck	das Ohr	ear
laufen	running	der Onkel	uncle
laut	loud	orange	orange (color)

German-English Word List

die Orange	orange (fruit)	das Sandwich	sandwich
die Overalls	overalls	sauber	clean
der Panda	panda	das Schaf	sheep
das Pferd	horse	der Schal	scarf
die Pfanne	pan	die Schere	scissors
die Pfannkuchen	pancakes	das Schiff	ship
pfeifen	whistle	die Schildkröte	turtle
der Pinguin	penguin	die Schlafanzüge	pajamas
die Pizza	pizza	schlafen	sleeping
die Plätzchen	cookies	das Schlafzimmer	bedroom
das Polizeiauto	police car	die Schlange	snake
die Pommes	chips	das Schlittschuhlaufen	skating
die Pommes frites	french fries	die Schnecke	snail
das Popcorn	popkorn	der Schnee	snow
prallen	bounce	schmutzig	dirty
der Pullover	sweater	der Schneebesen	whisk
das Pult	desk	das Schneidebrett	cutting board
das Quadrat	square	die Schuhe	shoes
die Rakete	rocket	der Schulbus	school bus
der Rechner	calculator	die Schule	school
das Rechteck	rectangle	die Schülerin	student (female)
reden	talking	die Schulter	shoulder
der Regen	rain	die Schüssel	bowl
der Regenbogen	rainbow	der Schwamm	sponge
der Reis	rice	schwarz	black
der Rock	skirt	das Schwein	pig
der Roller	scooter	schwer	heavy
rosa	pink	die Schwester	sister
rot	red	sechs	six
der Rucksack	backpack	segeln	sailing
ruhig	quiet	die Seife	soap
der Salat	salad	das Shampoo	shampoo

German-English Word List

sieben	seven	die Toilette	toilet
sitzen	sit	das Toilettenpapier	toilet paper
die Skala	scale	die Tomate	tomato
das Skateboard	skateboard	der Topf	pot
die Socken	socks	der Traktor	tractor
der Sommer	summer	der Transport	transportation
die Sonne	sun	der Tornado	tornado
die Sonnenbrille	sunglasses	traurig	sad
die Spaghetti	spaghetti	die Treppe	stairs
der Spiegel	mirror	trinken	drinking
der Sport	sports	trocken	dry
springen	jump	der Truthahn	turkey
die Spüle	sink	T-Shirt	t-shirt
stark	strong	die Tür	door
stehen	standing	die Turnschuhe	sneakers
die Stiefel	boots	über	above
die Stirn	forehead	überrascht	surprised
die Strumpfhose	tights	die Uhr	clock
der Stern	star	umarmen	hugging
der Stuhl	chair	unten	below
das Sweatshirt	sweatshirt	unten	down
der Tacker	stapler	das Unterseeboot	submarine
die Tante	aunt	die Unterwäsche	underwear
die Tasse	cup	der Vater	father
die Teekanne	teapot	vier	four
der Teller	plate	der Vogel	bird
das Tennis	tennis	der Wagen	wagon
der Tennisschläger	tennis racket	der Wal	whale
die Tiere	animals	die Wange	cheek
der Tiger	tiger	der Wasserhahn	faucet
der Tisch	table	der Wasserkessel	kettle
der Toast	toast	die Wassermelone	watermelon

German-English Word List

weich	soft
weinen	cry
weiß	white
wütend	angry
das Wetter	weather
der Wind	wind
der Winter	winter
das Wohnzimmer	living room
der Wolf	wolf
die Wolke	cloud
die Zahnbürste	toothbrush
die Zahnpasta	toothpaste
das Zebra	zebra
der Zeh	toe
zehn	ten
die Ziege	goat
ziehen	pull
die Zitrone	lemon
der Zug	train
zwei	two
die Zwiebel	onion

English-German Word List

above	über	bookcase	das Bücherregal
action words	das Aktionsverb	boots	die Stiefel
afraid	ängstlich	bounce	prallen
alligator	der Alligator	bowl	die Schüssel
alphabet	das Alphabet	boxing	boxen
ambulance	der Krankenwagen	bread	das Brot
angry	wütend	broccoli	der Brokkoli
animals	die Tiere	brother	der Bruder
apple	der Apfel	brush	die Bürste
arm	der Arm	bubbles	die Blasen
aunt	die Tante	bus	der Bus
autumn	der Herbst	butter	die Butter
backpack	der Rucksack	cake	der Kuchen
banana	die Banane	calculator	der Rechner
baseball	der Baseball	camel	das Kamel
basketball	der Basketball	car	das Auto
bathroom	das Badezimmer	carrot	die Karotte
bathtub	die Badewanne	cat	die Katze
bear	der Bär	chair	der Stuhl
bed	das Bett	cheek	die Wange
bedroom	das Schlafzimmer	cheese	der Käse
below	unten	chest	die Brust
belt	der Gürtel	chicken	das Hühnerfleisch
bicycle	das Fahrrad	chin	das Kinn
bird	der Vogel	chips	die Pommes
black	schwarz	circle	der Kreis
blanket	die Decke	clean	sauber
blouse	die Bluse	climbing	klettern
blue	blau	clock	die Uhr
boat	das Boot	closed	geschlossen
body	der Körper	clothes	die Kleidung
book	das Buch	cloud	die Wolke

English-German Word List

English	German		English	German
coat	der Mantel		eight	acht
cold	kalt		elbow	der Ellbogen
colors	die Farben		elephant	der Elefant
comb	der Kamm		emotions	die Emotionen
cookies	die Plätzchen		eye	das Auge
corn	der Mais		eyebrow	die Augenbraue
couch	die Couch		face	das Gesicht
cousin (male)	der Cousin		family	die Familie
cousin (female)	die Kusine		father	der Vater
cow	die Kuh		faucet	der Wasserhahn
crawling	kriechen		finger	der Finger
crayons	die Buntstifte		fire truck	das Feuerwehrauto
cry	weinen		fireplace	der Kamin
cup	die Tasse		fish	der Fisch
curious	neugierig		fishing	angeln
cutting board	das Schneidebrett		five	fünf
dark	dunkel		food	das Essen
desk	das Pult		foot	der Fuß
diamond	der Diamant		football	der Fußball
dirty	schmutzig		forehead	die Stirn
dishwasher	die Geschirrspüler		fork	die Gabel
dog	der Hund		fox	der Fuchs
door	die Tür		four	vier
down	unten		french fries	die Pommes frites
dress	das Kleid		frog	der Frosch
dresser	die Frisierkommode		giraffe	die Giraffe
drinking	trinken		glass	das Glas
dry	trocken		globe	der Globus
duck	die Ente		glove	der Handschuh
ear	das Ohr		glue	der Klebstoff
eating	Essen		goat	die Ziege
egg	das Ei		golf	golf

English-German Word List

gorilla	der Gorilla	light	das Licht
grandfather	der Großvater	light	leicht
grandmother	dee Großmutter	lightning	der Blitz
green	grün	lion	der Löwe
groceries	die Lebensmittel	listening	hören
hair	die Haare	living room	das Wohnzimmer
hand	die Hand	loud	laut
happy	glücklich	microwave	die Mikrowelle
hard	hart	milk	die Milch
hat	der Hut	mirror	der Spiegel
head	der Kopf	monkey	der Affe
heavy	schwer	moose	der Elch
helicopter	der Hubschrauber	mother	die Mutter
hippopotamus	das Nilpferd	motorcycle	das Motorrad
horse	das Pferd	mouse	die Maus
hot	heiß	mouth	der Mund
house	das Haus	neck	der Hals
hugging	umarmen	necktie	die Krawatte
ice cream	die Eiscreme	nine	neun
jacket	die Jacke	nose	die Nase
jeans	die Jeans	notebooks	die Notizbücher
jump	springen	numbers	die Nummern
karate	karate	nuts	die Nüsse
kettle	der Wasserkessel	old	alt
kitchen	die Küche	one	eins
knee	das Knie	onion	die Zwiebel
knife	das Messer	open	öffnen
lamp	die Lampe	opposites	die Gegensätze
laugh	lachen	orange (color)	orange
leg	das Bein	orange (fruit)	die Orange
lemon	die Zitrone	overalls	die Overalls
library	die Bibliothek	owl	die Eule

English-German Word List

paint	die Farbe		rocket	die Rakete
pajamas	die Schlafanzüge		rooster	der Hahn
pan	die Pfanne		ruler	das Lineal
pancakes	die Pfannkuchen		running	laufen
panda	der Panda		sad	traurig
pants	die Hosen		sailing	segeln
pear	die Birne		salad	der Salat
pen	der Kugelschreiber		sandwich	das Sandwich
pencil	der Bleistift		scale	die Skala
penguin	der Pinguin		scarf	der Schal
pig	das Schwein		school	die Schule
pillow	das Kissen		school bus	der Schulbus
pink	rosa		scissors	die Schere
pizza	die Pizza		scooter	der Roller
plate	der Teller		seasons	die Jahreszeiten
police car	das Polizeiauto		seven	sieben
popkorn	das Popcorn		shampoo	das Shampoo
pot	der Topf		shapes	die Formen
potatoes	die Kartoffeln		sheep	das Schaf
pull	ziehen		ship	das Schiff
purple	lila		shirt	das Hemd
purse	die Handtasche		shoes	die Schuhe
push	drücken		shoulder	die Schulter
quiet	ruhig		shower	die Dusche
rabbit	das Kaninchen		sink	die Spüle
rain	der Regen		sister	die Schwester
rainbow	der Regenbogen		sit	sitzen
read	lesen		six	sechs
rectangle	das Rechteck		skateboard	das Skateboard
red	rot		skating	das Schlittschuhlaufen
refrigerator	der Kühlschrank		skirt	der Rock
rice	der Reis		sleeping	schlafen

English-German Word List

snail	die Schnecke	swimsuit	der Badeanzug
snake	die Schlange	swim trunks	die Badehose
sneakers	die Turnschuhe	table	der Tisch
snow	der Schnee	talking	reden
soap	die Seife	teacher	die Lehrerin
soccer	der Fußball	teapot	die Teekanne
socks	die Socken	television	der Fernseher
soft	weich	ten	zehn
spaghetti	die Spaghetti	tennis	das Tennis
sponge	der Schwamm	tennis racket	der Tennisschläger
spoon	der Löffel	three	drei
sports	der Sport	tiger	der Tiger
spring	der Frühling	tights	die Strumpfhose
square	das Quadrat	tissue	das Gewebe
squirrel	das Eichhörnchen	toast	der Toast
stairs	die Treppe	toe	der Zeh
standing	stehen	toilet	die Toilette
stapler	der Tacker	toilet paper	das Toilettenpapier
star	der Stern	tomato	die Tomate
stomach	der Magen	toothbrush	die Zahnbürste
stool	der Hocker	toothpaste	die Zahnpasta
stove	der Herd	tornado	der Tornado
strawberries	die Erdbeeren	towel	das Handtuch
strong	stark	tractor	der Traktor
student	die Schülerin	train	der Zug
submarine	das Unterseeboot	transportation	der Transport
summer	der Sommer	triangle	das Dreieck
sun	die Sonne	truck	der Lastwagen
sunglasses	die Sonnenbrille	t-shirt	das T-Shirt
surprised	überrascht	turkey	der Truthahn
sweater	der Pullover	turtle	die Schildkröte
sweatshirt	das Sweatshirt	two	zwei

English-German Word List

uncle	der Onkel		**whisper**	flüstern
underwear	die Unterwäsche		**whistle**	pfeifen
up	oben		**white**	weiß
wagon	der Wagen		**wind**	der Wind
walking	gehen		**window**	das Fenster
wardrobe	der Kleiderschrank		**winter**	der Winter
watermelon	die Wassermelone		**wolf**	der Wolf
weather	das Wetter		**wrist**	das Handgelenk
wet	nass		**yellow**	gelb
whale	der Wal		**young**	jung
whisk	der Schneebesen		**zebra**	das Zebra

Published by Dylanna Press an imprint of Dylanna Publishing, Inc.
Copyright © 2021 by Dylanna Press

Editor: Julie Grady